~only God can make a tree

~a Meditation~

English Hill Books

Copyright © Peter Grimord

First Printing 2020
Edited by Erroll Imre

Poems, parts of poems, and quotes appearing in this book
are from the public domain or used under the guidelines
of the fair use doctrine.

All rights reserved. Artwork in this book may not be reproduced
or transmitted in any form or by any means whatsoever
without express permission from the artist.

This Book
is dedicated to:
Barbara A. Grimord,
my mother, who sighed
with relief when I
told her I was going
to be an artist.

Growing up I didn't want to be an artist because I knew it would be a monumental stone to pull, and my decision to go to art school surprised nobody but myself.

My Story

Welcome to my world of Pen and Ink, a traditional art that is as old as history. Drawing is something I've done since I could hold a pen, and stippling is a technique I taught myself when making laboratory drawings for biology while in college. My professors told me to go into medical illustration, but this idea went nowhere with me, and I decided to go to art school instead. The years after graduation led to a career as a sculptor and photographer, doing contemporary work that reflected the urban environment of Philadelphia, where my wife, also an artist, and I lived for 24 years after leaving the midwestern college town of our birth. I had forsaken drawing until our small family moved to rural Pennsylvania in 2004, where I slowly re-acquainted myself with my love of looking at natural subjects. After a brief time teaching drawing in the local schools, I bought a set of Rapidograph technical fountain pens and began to draw.

The title of my book comes from the words of Joyce Kilmer in his poem called *Trees*. The entire poem is on the next page.

January 16, 2020

Trees

I think I shall never see
A poem lovely as a tree.

A tree whose hungry mouth is prest
Against the earth's sweet flowing breast;

A tree that looks at God all day,
And lifts her leafy arms to pray;

A tree that may in Summer wear
A nest of robins in her hair;

Upon whose bosom snow has lain;
Who intimately lives with rain.

Poems are made by fools like me,
But only God can make a tree.

Plate 1.

Plate 2.

Man cannot afford to be
a naturalist,
to look at Nature
directly,
but only with
the side of his eye.
He must look
through and beyond her.

-Henry David Thoreau

Plate 3.

Plate 4.

Between every two pine trees there is a door leading to a new way of life.

—John Muir

Plate 5.

Plate 6.

Trees Need Not Walk the Earth

Trees need not walk the earth
For beauty or for bread;
Beauty will come to them
Where they stand.
Here among the children of the sap
Is no pride of ancestry:
A birch may wear no less the morning
Than an oak.
Here are no heirlooms
Save those of loveliness,
In which each tree
Is kingly in its heritage of grace.
Here is but beauty's wisdom
In which all trees are wise.
Trees need not walk the earth
For beauty or for bread;
Beauty will come to them
In the rainbow-
The sunlight-
And the lilac-haunted rain;
And bread will come to them
As beauty came:
In the rainbow-
In the sunlight-
In the rain.

-David Rosenthal

Plate 7.

Plate 8.

My November Guest

My Sorrow, when she's here with me,
Thinks these dark days of autumn rain
Are beautiful as days can be;
She loves the bare, the withered tree;
She walks the sodden pasture lane.

Her pleasure will not let me stay.
She talks and I am fain to list:
She's glad the birds are gone away,
She's glad her simple worsted grey
Is silver now with clinging mist.

The desolate, deserted trees,
The faded earth, the heavy sky,
The beauties she so truly sees,
She thinks I have no eye for these,
And vexes me for reason why.

Not yesterday I learned to know
The love of bare November days
Before the coming of the snow,
But it were vain to tell her so,
And they are better for her praise.

-Robert Frost

Plate 9.

Plate 10.

To me, nature is sacred. Trees are my temples and forests are my cathedrals.

-Mikhail Gorbachev

Plate 11.

Plate 12.

If there is any one duty which more than another we owe it to our children and our children's children to perform at once, it is to save the forests of this country, for they constitute the first and most important element in the conservation of the natural resources of the country.

-Theodore Roosevelt

Plate 13.

Plate 14.

I begin to see an object when I cease to understand it.

-Henry David Thoreau

Plate 15.

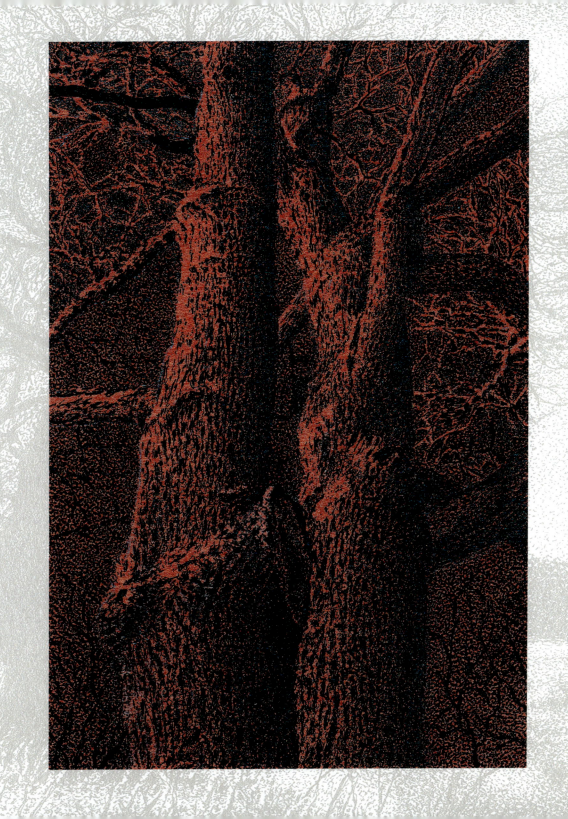

Plate 16.

Plate 17.

I'd rather be in the mountains thinking of God, than in church thinking about the mountains.

—John Muir

Plate 18.

Plate 19.

That sort of beauty which is called natural,
as of vines, plants, trees, etc.,
consists of a very complicated harmony;
and all the natural motions, and tendencies,
and figures of the bodies in the universe
are done according to proportion,
and therein is their beauty.

-Jonathan Edwards
Theologian

Plate 20.

Plate 21.

Adversity

A barren field o'ergrown with thorn and weed
It stays for him who waits for help from God:
Only the soul that makes a plough of Need
Shall know what blossoms underneath its sod.

-Madison Julius Cawein

Plate 22.

Plate 23.

The Oak

Live thy life,
Young and old,
Like yon oak,
Bright in spring,
Living gold;

Summer-rich
Then; and then
Autumn-changed
Soberer-hued
Gold again.

All his leaves
Fall'n at length,
Look, he stands,
Trunk and bough
Naked strength.

-Alfred Lord Tennyson

Plate 24.

Plate 25.

My profession
is to always find God
in nature.

-Henry David Thoreau

Plate 26.

Plate 27.

Desert Places

Snow falling and night falling fast, oh, fast
In a field I looked into going past,
And the ground almost covered smooth in snow,
But a few weeds and stubble showing last.

The woods around it have it, it is theirs.
All animals are smothered in their lairs.
I am too absent-spirited to count;
The loneliness includes me unawares.

And lonely as it is, that loneliness
Will be more lonely ere it will be less
A blanker whiteness of benighted snow
With no expression, nothing to express.

They cannot scare me with their empty spaces
Between stars, on stars where no human race is.
I have it in me so much nearer home
To scare myself with my own desert places.

-Robert Frost

Plate 28.

Plate 29.

The happiest man
is he who learns
from nature
the lesson of worship.

-Ralph Waldo Emerson

Plate 30.

Plate 31.

Winter Trees

All the complicated details
of the attiring and
the disattiring are completed!
A liquid moon
moves gently among
the long branches.
Thus having prepared their buds
against a sure winter
the wise trees
stand sleeping in the cold.

William Carlos Williams

Plate 32.

Plate 33.

I never before knew
the full value of trees.
Under them I breakfast,
dine, write, read
and receive my company.

-Thomas Jefferson

Plate 34.

Plate 35.

The earth is at the same time mother,
She is mother of all that is natural,
mother of all that is human.
She is the mother of all,
for contained in her are the seeds of all.

The earth of humankind
contains all moistness, all verdancy,
all germinating power.
It is in so many ways fruitful.
All creation comes from it.

Yet it forms not only the basic
raw material for mankind,
but also the substance of the incarnation
of God's son.

-Saint Hildegard of Bingen

Plate 36.

Plate 37.

The health of the eye
seems to demand a horizon.
We are never tired,
as long as we can see
far enough.

-Ralph Waldo Emerson

Plate 38.

Plate 39.

In the depths
of winter,
I finally learned
that within me
there lay an
invincible summer.

-Albert Camus

We've arrived at the end of the first book of a planned series that will include my entire oeuvre of pen and inks. Please watch for these online at English Hill Books, our private publishing house, which has books by my wife, Joan Gallup Grimord. I can be contacted by email at petejoan@ptdprolog.net or pgrimord@gmail.com. Also, I sell limited edition fine reproductions of my drawings, printed in my studio at original dimensions, on cotton rag paper similar to that on which I draw. These are available framed or matted. As for the original drawings, I hope to find a permanent home where they will be appropriately handled and given a public venue so my technique, a slow and tedious process, may inspire future artists and keep alive the twin virtues of patience and beauty that we inherited from our classical forebearers. Any ideas are welcome.

I would like to complete Book One by quoting the final few lines of a poem by John Greenleaf Whittier called Questions of Life:

From Nature, and her mockery, Art;
And book and speech of men apart,
To the still witness in my heart;
With reverence waiting to behold
His Avatar of love untold,
The Eternal Beauty new and old

plates

1. 2016. *Sycamore Tree.* I see this tree every time I drive the route between Bloomsburg and Williamsport.

2. 2016. *Doris' Lone Tree on Lilac Paper.* Doris is our neighbor, and her family has been in the same house for several generations. I have drawn many trees that stand on or near her property.

3. 2018. *Runnymede Tree.* Runnymede is a small nature and cultural center located on an old farm east of State College, PA. While visiting and hanging my drawings for exhibition in the gallery, I spent a few hours photographing trees on the surrounding acreage and found this oddly shaped specimen.

4. 2019. *Doris' Tree on Deep Green.* Another tree I associate with my neighbor's legacy.

5. 2015. *Pine Forest Undergrowth.* I found this tree on the land alongside a lake owned by a regional power generation plant.

6. 2016. *White Pines at Ikler Cemetery on Rose Paper.* Old trees on an ancient burial ground.

7. 2018. *Midwestern Sky Over the Mississippi River.* I saw this while driving to Little Rock for an art exhibition.

8. 2015. *Estuary Shoreline on the South Carolina coast.*

9. 2014. *Sky Over Walnut Branches.* I found this tree not far from the white pines grove described in Plate #5.

10. 2015. *Hedgerow Trees Near Danville.* This row of trees divides farmland from residential properties and is a perfect example of what I call *braiding*. I notice this growth pattern when trees are in rows, and a curious twist emerges as the thin trunks spiral their way into the sky. I don't know what it is, or even if it is anything at all.

11. 2018. *Clouds Over the Hill.* As the title implies, I am looking through a sparse row of trees that line a ridge overlooking the expansive Susquehanna River Valley.

12. 2016. *Trees at the End of Bear Trail.* I enjoy riding my bicycle on logging roads and this view greets me at the end of a trail I dubbed Bear Trail due to my observing a large black bear running up a heavily wooded slope that follows the path.

13. 2015. *A Very Cold Day in February on Lilac Paper.*

14. 2015. *March Thaw.* On this day, the air was heavy with moisture as the snow melted.

15. 2014. *Walnuts in the Moonlight.* With pen and ink, it is easy to lose detail when rendering dark subjects. I let the paper's dark tone help me keep the bark definable while not losing the moonlit impression.

16. 2015. *Bunny Patch.* Rabbits like this kind of place, and so do I.

17. 2015. *The Blue Ridge Mountains in February on Lilac Paper.* I found this tortured and lonely looking tree high in the Virginia mountains.

18. 2018. *Lehigh Valley Tree.* I believe this drawing captures the classical Pennsylvania landscape: a layered wedding cake of mountain ridges that melts into the sky with a minimal distinction between earth and atmosphere. Everything blends together.

19. 2019. *Vertigo Tree.* Here is my experiment in rendering a foreshortened standing tree.

20. 2019. *Hidden Tree Stump.* In the lower left-hand corner is a grassy bump where a tree stood not too long ago. This is a weed tree stump; I call them scrub willows found on farmland and are often removed by the farmers when they get in the way. No blame on the farmers, they have a hard job, but I try to capture these fascinating trees before they disappear.

21. 2019. *Live Oak.* I found this in North Carolina while on a path in wooded parkland. It was prehistoric in scale and fun to draw. I have another view of this tree later in this volume.

22. 2017. *Powerlines Farm Trees.* Here are two trees, one big tree, and one dwarf, situated east of Lewisburg on a farm that names itself after an array of powerlines that pass over the property. I exercised the artist's preference and left out the dark and heavy electric wires.

23. 2014. *Tall Lone White Pine.* This elegant tree is on the southwest corner of my property, and I see it every day. This drawing was done early after my return to pen and ink.

24. 2015. *White Oak on Rose Paper.* I pass this tree when hiking or riding my bike on a gravel farm trail called Morrison Road. It is an archetypal specimen of the Oak Tree and will be the subject of future drawings.

25. 2019. *Tree on Tractor Trails.* As a drawer, I often minimize traces of modern human activity in the subject matter to nudge the finished drawing a little bit closer to an imagined primordial landscape. Leaving the tractor marks in the grass is a self-imposed affront to this romantic impulse, a difference only my wife would notice, and did.

26. 2017. *Two Hardwoods.* Horse grazing keeps the grass around these trees cropped year-round and makes for a perfect view of them and their February shadows.

27. 2018. *Orangeville.* Beneath the morning fog is the small town of Orangeville. From an overlook where powerlines make an opening in the thick forest, I made a drawing with trees clothed in summer leaves, something I rarely do.

28. 2016. *Fishing Creek Near Orangeville.* We live on a hilltop with tributaries for Fishing Creek running both north and south of where our home is; creeks surround us, which we notice when the floodwaters rise.

29. 2019. *Doris' Gothic Tree on Lilac Paper.* Here is one of many drawings of scrubby farm trees located near our neighbor's property. They ooze with character and are the subjects used in many of my pictures.

30. 2019. *Doris' Ridge Trees on Warm Grey Paper.* These trees stand behind the Gothic Tree in Plate #29.

31. 2018. *Twin Norway Spruce Trees.* These two trees stand alongside a man-made pond recently constructed on a property where I frequently pass on my backwoods bike rides. The trees long pre-date the pond and tower high over the newly landscaped surrounding area.

32. 2016. *Doris' Cut-down Scrub Willow.* This tree once stood amongst a reasonably expansive group of similar trees, many still standing and documented here in these pages. An arborist who saw my work at a Williamsport outdoor street show identified the tree pictured here as a species of willow, the numerous shoot-like thin branches being the best indicator. These trees look "fuzzy" from a distance.

33. 2017. *Doris' Diversion.* Standing alone in the upper left-hand corner of the drawing is the now missing tree described in Plate #32.

34. 2016. *Watsontown Along the Susquehanna River.* Three old sycamore trees line a high bank along the Susquehanna. The river is behind and below the trees.

35. 2019. *A Pine and a Hardwood in the Lehigh Valley.* These trees were a very short distance from the one described in Plate #18. Both scenes share the same atmosphere.

36. 2019. *Live Oak on Lilac Paper.* Here is a second drawing of the live oak in Plate #21.

37. 2016. *Pines in Ikler Cemetery on Lilac Paper.* Cemeteries and large old trees share the same ground and persist in a person's memory. Also, see Plate #6.

38. 2016. *Barn Fire.* An old barn on this site burned to the ground and left these trees, one dead and one barely alive, standing.

39. 2015. *Trees on a Very Cold Day.* The air was as brittle as those trees looked on that cold day in January.

Made in the USA
Middletown, DE
31 October 2021